science for a changing world

Prepared in cooperation with the U.S. Army Corps of Engineers

Total Dissolved Gas and Water Temperature in the Lower Columbia River, Oregon and Washington, Water Year 2012: Quality-Assurance Data and Comparison to Water-Quality Standards

By Dwight Q. Tanner, Heather M. Bragg, and Matthew W. Johnston

Open-File Report 2012–1256

U.S. Department of the Interior
U.S. Geological Survey

U.S. Department of the Interior
SALLY JEWELL, Secretary

U.S. Geological Survey
Suzette M. Kimball, Acting Director

U.S. Geological Survey, Reston, Virginia: 2013

For more information on the USGS—the Federal source for science about the Earth, its natural and living resources, natural hazards, and the environment, visit *http://www.usgs.gov* or call 1-888-ASK-USGS.

For an overview of USGS information products, including maps, imagery, and publications, visit *http://www.usgs.gov/pubprod*

To order this and other USGS information products, visit *http://store.usgs.gov*

Suggested citation:
Tanner, D.Q., Bragg, H.M., and Johnston, M.W., 2013, Total dissolved gas and water temperature in the lower Columbia River, Oregon and Washington, water year 2012—Quality-assurance data and comparison to water-quality standards: U.S. Geological Survey Open-File Report 2012–1256, 26 p.

The use of trade, product, or firm names is for descriptive purposes only and does not imply endorsement by the U.S. Government.

Although this report is in the public domain, permission must be secured from the individual copyright owners to reproduce any copyrighted material contained within this report.

Contents

Significant Findings 1

Introduction 1

    Background 2

    Purpose and Scope 3

Methods of Data Collection 5

Completeness and Quality of Data for Total Dissolved Gas 5

Quality-Assurance Data 7

Effects of Spill on Concentration of Total Dissolved Gas 10

Comparison of Total-Dissolved-Gas Concentration and Water Temperature to Water-Quality Standards 12

Acknowledgments 25

References Cited 25

Figures

Figure 1. Location of U.S. Army Corp of Engineers dams and total-dissolved-gas monitoring stations, lower Columbia River, Oregon and Washington, water year 2012. 2

Figure 2. Boxplot showing accuracy of total-dissolved-gas sensors in the laboratory after 3 or 4 weeks of field deployment at eight monitoring stations in the lower Columbia River, Oregon and Washington, water year 2012. 8

Figure 3. Boxplot showing difference between the secondary standard and the field barometers in the field after 3 or 4 weeks of field deployment at eight stations in the lower Columbia River, Oregon and Washington, water year 2012. 9

Figure 4. Boxplot showing difference between the secondary standard and the field temperature instruments in the field after 3 or 4 weeks of field deployment at eight stations in the lower Columbia River, Oregon and Washington, water year 2012. 9

Figure 5. Boxplot showing difference between the secondary standard and the field total-dissolved-gas instruments in the field after 3 or 4 weeks of field deployment at eight stations in the lower Columbia River, Oregon and Washington, water year 2012. 10

Figure 6. Graph showing relation of total-dissolved-gas saturation downstream of John Day Dam and spill from the dam, lower Columbia River, Oregon and Washington, April 1–August 31, 2012 10

Figure 7. Graph showing relation of total-dissolved-gas saturation downstream of The Dalles Dam and spill from The Dalles Dam, lower Columbia River, Oregon and Washington, April 1–August 31, 2012. 11

Figure 8. Graph showing relation of total-dissolved-gas saturation downstream of Bonneville Dam at Cascade Island and spill from Bonneville Dam, lower Columbia River, Oregon and Washington, April 1–August 31, 2012....11

Figure 9. Graph showing relation of total-dissolved-gas saturation downstream of Bonneville Dam at Warrendale and spill from Bonneville Dam, lower Columbia River, Oregon and Washington, April 1–August 31, 2012 12

Figure 10. Boxplot showing distributions of hourly total-dissolved-gas data and Oregon and Washington total-dissolved-gas waivers/rule adjustments, lower Columbia River, Oregon and Washington, April 1–August 31, 2012.13

Figure 11. Graphs showing high 12-hour average of total-dissolved-gas saturation at John Day Dam navigation lock and spill from McNary Dam, lower Columbia River, Oregon and Washington, April 1–August 31, 2012 14

Figure 12. Graphs showing total-dissolved-gas saturation at John Day Dam tailwater and spill from John Day Dam, lower Columbia River, Oregon and Washington, April 1–August 31, 2012..15

Figure 13. Graphs showing total-dissolved-gas saturation at The Dalles Dam forebay and spill from John Day Dam, lower Columbia River, Oregon and Washington, April 1–August 31, 2012..16

Figure 14. Graphs showing total-dissolved-gas saturation at The Dalles Dam tailwater and spill from The Dalles Dam, lower Columbia River, Oregon and Washington, April 1–August 31, 2012...17

Figure 15. Graphs showing total-dissolved-gas saturation at Bonneville Dam forebay and spill from The Dalles Dam, lower Columbia River, Oregon and Washington, April 1–August 31, 2012..18

Figure 16. Graphs showing total-dissolved-gas saturation at Cascade Island and spill from Bonneville Dam, lower Columbia River, Oregon and Washington, April 1–August 31, 2012..19

Figure 17. Graphs showing total-dissolved-gas saturation at Warrendale and spill from Bonneville Dam, lower Columbia River, Oregon and Washington, April 1–August 31, 2012..20

Figure 18. Graphs showing total-dissolved-gas saturation at Camas and spill from Bonneville Dam, lower Columbia River, Oregon and Washington, April 1–August 31, 2012..21

Figure 19. Graph showing water temperature upstream of John Day Dam and downstream of John Day Dam, lower Columbia River, Oregon and Washington, summer 2012...22

Figure 20. Graph showing water temperature upstream and downstream of The Dalles Dam, lower Columbia River, Oregon and Washington, summer 2012...23

Figure 21. Graph showing water temperature upstream of Bonneville Dam and downstream of Bonneville Dam at Cascade Island, lower Columbia River, Oregon and Washington, summer 2012...23

Figure 22. Graph showing water temperature upstream of Bonneville Dam and downstream of Bonneville Dam at Warrendale, lower Columbia River, Oregon and Washington, summer 2012...24

Figure 23. Graph showing water temperature downstream of Bonneville Dam at Camas, lower Columbia River, Oregon and Washington, summer 2012...24

Tables

Table 1. Total-dissolved-gas monitoring stations, lower Columbia River, Oregon and Washington, water year 2012 4

Table 2. Completeness and quality of total-dissolved gas data, lower Columbia River, Oregon and Washington, water year 2012 6

Table 3. Periods of missing real-time TDG data, lower Columbia River, Oregon and Washington, water year 2012 7

Conversion Factors, Datum, and Abbreviations and Acronyms

Conversion Factors

Multiply	By	To obtain
cubic foot per second (ft^3/s)	0.02832	cubic meter per second (m^3/s)
mile (mi)	1.609	kilometer (km)
millimeter (mm)	0.03937	inch (in.)
square mile (mi^2)	2.590	square kilometer (km^2)

Temperature in degrees Celsius (°C) may be converted to degrees Fahrenheit (°F) as follows: °F=(1.8×°C)+32.

Datum

Horizontal coordinate information is referenced to the North American Datum of 1927 (NAD 27).

Abbreviations and Acronyms

BON	Bonneville forebay
CCIW	Cascade Island
CWMW	Camas
DCP	Data-collection platform
GOES	Geostationary Operational Environmental Satellite
JDY	John Day navigation lock
JHAW	John Day Dam tailwater
NIST	National Institute of Standards and Technology
RM	River mile
TDA	The Dalles forebay
TDDO	The Dalles tailwater
TDG	Total dissolved gas
USACE	U.S. Army Corps of Engineers
USGS	U.S. Geological Survey
WRNO	Warrendale

Total Dissolved Gas and Water Temperature in the Lower Columbia River, Oregon and Washington, Water Year 2012: Quality-Assurance Data and Comparison to Water-Quality Standards

By Dwight Q. Tanner, Heather M. Bragg, and Matthew W. Johnston

Significant Findings

Air is entrained in water as it is flows through the spillways of dams, which causes an increase in the concentration of total dissolved gas in the water downstream from the dams. The elevated concentrations of total dissolved gas can adversely affect fish and other freshwater aquatic life. An analysis of total-dissolved-gas and water-temperature data collected at eight monitoring stations on the lower Columbia River in Oregon and Washington in 2012 indicated the following:

- During parts of the spill season of April–August 2012, hourly values of total dissolved gas (TDG) were larger than 115-percent saturation for the forebay stations (John Day navigation lock, The Dalles forebay, and Bonneville forebay) and the Camas station. Hourly values of total dissolved gas were larger than 120-percent saturation for the tailwater stations (John Day Dam tailwater, The Dalles tailwater, Cascade Island, and Warrendale).

- During parts of August and September 2012, hourly water temperatures were greater than 20°C (degrees Celsius) at the eight stations on the lower Columbia River. According to the State of Oregon water-temperature standard, the 7-day average of the daily maximum temperature of the lower Columbia River should not exceed 20°C; Washington regulations state that the 1-day maximum should not exceed 20°C as a result of human activities.

- Of the 98 laboratory TDG checks that were performed on instruments after field deployment, all were within ± 0.7-percent saturation.

- All but 1 of the 83 field checks of TDG sensors with a secondary standard were within ± 1.0-percent saturation after 3–4 weeks of deployment in the river. All 88 of the field checks of barometric pressure were within ±1 millimeter of mercury of a primary standard, and all 85 water-temperature field checks were within ±0.2°C of a secondary standard.

- For the eight monitoring stations in water year 2012, a total of 97.0 percent of the TDG data were received in real time and were within 1-percent saturation of the expected value on the basis of calibration data, replicate quality-control measurements in the river, and comparison to ambient river conditions at adjacent sites. Data received from the Cascade Island site were only 77.8 percent complete because the equipment was destroyed by high water. The other stations ranged from 98.9 to 100.0 percent complete.

Introduction

The U.S. Army Corps of Engineers (USACE) operates several dams in the lower Columbia River Basin in Oregon and Washington (fig. 1), which encompasses 259,000 mi^2 of the Pacific Northwest. These dams are multipurpose structures that fill regional needs for flood control, navigation, irrigation, recreation, hydropower production, fish and wildlife habitat, water-quality maintenance, and municipal and industrial water supply. When water is released through the spillways of these dams (instead of being routed through the turbines to generate electricity), ambient air is entrained in the water, which results in an increase in the concentration of dissolved gases in the water (referred to here as "total dissolved gas," or TDG) downstream of the spillways. Concentrations of TDG greater than 110-percent saturation can cause gas-bubble trauma in fish and adversely affect other aquatic organisms (U.S. Environmental Protection Agency, 1986).

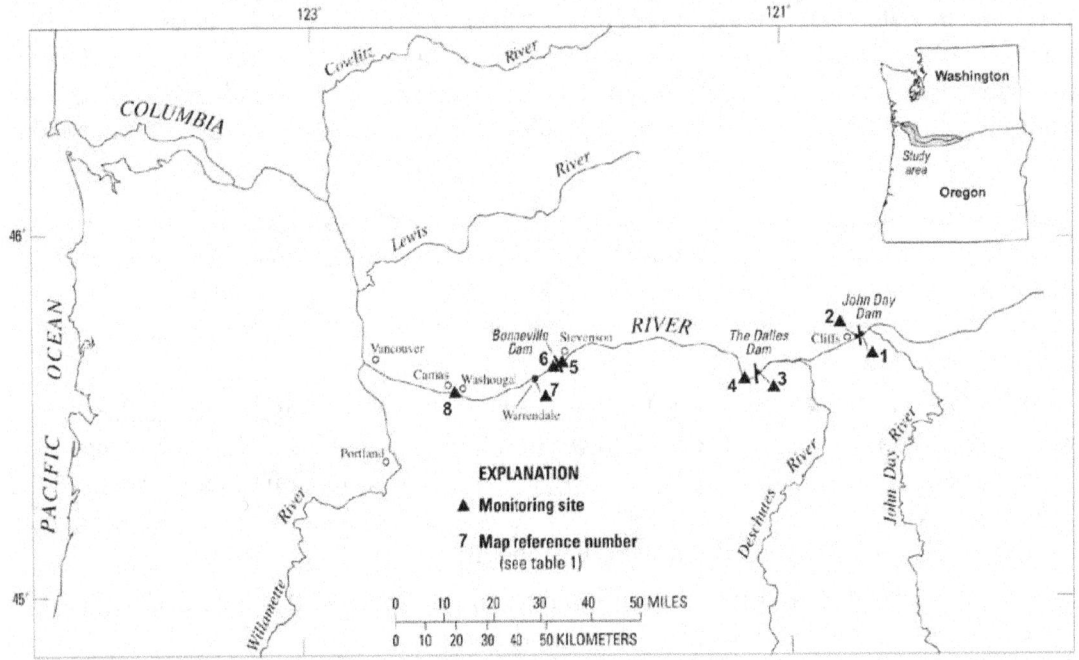

Base map modified from USGS and other digital data, variable scales. Projection unknown.

Figure 1. Location of U.S. Army Corp of Engineers dams and total-dissolved-gas monitoring stations, lower Columbia River, Oregon and Washington, water year 2012.

The USACE regulates streamflow and spill from its dams on the lower Columbia River to minimize the production of excess TDG downstream from the dams, with the additional goal of providing for fish passage through the spillways (rather than through the turbines). The States of Oregon and Washington issue waivers and rule adjustments, respectively, to the TDG water-quality standards during the spring and summer when the fish are migrating downstream. To monitor compliance, the USACE oversees the collection of real-time TDG and water-temperature data upstream and downstream of Columbia River Basin dams in a network of monitoring stations.

Background

Real-time TDG and water-temperature data are vital to the USACE for dam operation and for monitoring compliance with environmental regulations. The data are used by water managers to maintain water-quality conditions that facilitate fish passage and ensure their survival in the lower Columbia River. The U.S. Geological Survey (USGS), in cooperation with the Portland District of the USACE, has collected TDG and related data in the lower Columbia River each year since 1996. Those data are available online within an hour of collection time, and the current and historical TDG and water-temperature data can be accessed at *http://oregon.usgs.gov/projs_dir/pn307.tdg/* (accessed February 15, 2013). Thirteen reports, published for water years 1996 and 2000–2011, contain TDG data, quality-assurance data, and descriptions of the methods of data collection (Tanner and others, 1996; Tanner and Bragg, 2001; Tanner and Johnston, 2001; and Tanner and others, 2002, 2003, 2004, 2005, 2006, 2007, 2008, 2009, 2011, 2012).

To assure the accuracy and integrity of the data needed for managing and modeling TDG in the lower Columbia River, hourly values for 2012 were reviewed relative to laboratory and field measurements made during instrument calibrations and daily intersite comparisons. A small fraction of the TDG data was deleted because the data did not meet a ±1-percent criterion during quality control checks. The hourly values were stored in the USGS database and in a USACE database (U.S. Army Corps of Engineers, 2012). The USACE database also includes hourly river discharge and spill data.

Purpose and Scope

This report describes the TDG data and related quality-assurance data from eight monitoring stations on the lower Columbia River, from the navigation lock of the John Day Dam (river mile [RM] 215.7) to Camas, Washington (RM 121.7) (fig. 1, table 1). Data for water year 2012 (October 1, 2011–September 30, 2012) include hourly measurements of TDG pressure, barometric pressure, water temperature, and probe depth. Five of the stations (John Day Dam navigation lock, The Dalles Dam forebay, Bonneville Dam forebay, Cascade Island, and Camas) were operated from March through September 2012, the period that includes the usual time of spill from the dams. The stations John Day Dam tailwater, The Dalles Dam tailwater, and Warrendale were operated year-round.

Table 1. Total-dissolved-gas monitoring stations, lower Columbia River, Oregon and Washington, water year 2012.

[Map reference number refers to figure 1; USACE, U.S. Army Corps of Engineers; Columbia River mile locations were determined from U.S. Geological Survey (USGS) 7.5-minute topographic maps; stations in this report are referenced by their abbreviated name or USACE station identifier; °, degree; ′, minute; ″, second; latitude and longitude are referenced to the North American Datum of 1927; River mile is distance from the mouth of the Columbia River]

Map reference number	USACE station identifier	River mile	USGS station number	USGS station name (and abbreviated station name)	Latitude	Longitude	Period of record in water year 2012
1	JDY	215.7	454314120413701	Columbia River at John Day navigation lock, Washington (John Day navigation lock)	45° 43′ 14″	120° 41′ 37″	03/14/12–09/18/12
2	JHAW	214.7	454249120423500	Columbia River, right bank, near Cliffs, Washington (John Day tailwater)	45° 42′ 49″	120° 42′ 35″	Year-round
3	TDA	192.6	453712121071200	Columbia River at The Dalles Dam forebay, Washington (The Dalles forebay)	45° 37′ 12″	121° 07′ 12″	03/13/12–09/19/12
4	TDDO	188.9	14105700	Columbia River at The Dalles, Oregon (The Dalles tailwater)	45° 36′ 27″	121° 10′ 20″	Year-round
5	BON	146.1	453845121562000	Columbia River at Bonneville Dam forebay, Washington (Bonneville forebay)	45° 38′ 45″	121° 56′ 20″	03/14/12–09/19/12
6	CCIW	145.9	453845121564001	Columbia River at Cascade Island, Washington (Cascade Island)	45° 38′ 45″	121° 56′ 40″	03/07/12–04/25/12 and 06/06/12–09/19/12
7	WRNO	140.4	453630122021400	Columbia River, left bank, near Dodson, Oregon (Warrendale)	45° 36′ 30″	122° 02′ 14″	Year-round
8	CWMW	121.7	453439122223900	Columbia River, right bank, at Washougal, Washington (Camas)	45° 34′ 39″	122° 22′ 39″	03/08/12–09/03/12

Methods of Data Collection

Methods of data collection for TDG, barometric pressure, and water temperature are described in detail in Tanner and Johnston (2001). A summary of these methods follows: Instrumentation at each monitoring station consists of a Hach® Hydrolab water-quality probe, a Vaisala electronic barometer, a power supply, and a Sutron SatLink2 data-collection platform (DCP). The instruments at each station are powered by a 12-volt battery that is charged by a solar panel or a 120-volt alternating-current line. Measurements (including probe depth) are made, logged, and transmitted every hour. The DCP transmits the most recent logged data to the Geostationary Operational Environmental Satellite (GOES) system (Jones and others, 1991). The data are automatically decoded and transferred to the USACE and USGS databases.

The eight fixed-station monitors were calibrated every 3 weeks, except from October 2011 through March 2012, when they were calibrated at 4-week intervals. At the beginning of the monitoring season in March, a new TDG membrane was installed on each Hydrolab. The field calibration procedure was as follows: A Hydrolab (which was calibrated several days before the field trip and used as a secondary standard) was deployed alongside the field-deployed Hydrolab for a period of up to 1 hour to obtain check measurements of TDG and water temperature prior to removing the field Hydrolab (which had been deployed for 3 or 4 weeks). The field Hydrolab was then replaced with another Hydrolab that had been calibrated recently at the laboratory. The secondary standard was used again to check TDG and temperature measured by the newly deployed Hydrolab in the river. The equilibration process for the newly placed Hydrolab usually lasted about 1 hour. The electronic barometer at the fixed station was calibrated using a portable barometer (NovaLynx 230-M202) that had been calibrated to National Institute of Standards and Technology (NIST) standards.

During each field calibration, the minimum compensation depth was calculated to determine whether the Hydrolab was positioned at an appropriate depth to obtain an accurate measurement of TDG. This minimum compensation depth, which was calculated according to Colt (1984, p. 104), is the depth above which degassing will occur due to decreased hydrostatic pressure. To measure TDG accurately, the Hydrolabs were positioned, whenever possible, at a depth below the calculated minimum compensation depth.

The Hydrolab that was removed from the field after 3 or 4 weeks of deployment was then calibrated in the laboratory. The integrity of the TDG membrane was checked, and then the membrane was removed and air-dried. The TDG sensor (without the membrane attached) was calibrated at 0, 100, 200, and 300 mm Hg (millimeters of mercury) above atmospheric pressure to span the expected range of TDG in the river (approximately 100-, 113-, 126-, and 139-percent saturation, respectively).

Completeness and Quality of Data for Total Dissolved Gas

A summary of the completeness and quality of the TDG data for water year 2012 is shown in table 2. Data in table 2 were based on the total amount of hourly TDG pressure data that could have been collected during the monitoring season. The fourth column in table 2 shows the percentages of data that were received in real time and passed quality-assurance checks. TDG saturation values were considered to meet quality-assurance standards if they were within ±1-percent saturation of the expected value, based on calibration data, replicate quality-control measurements in the river, and daily comparisons to ambient river conditions at adjacent sites.

Table 2. Completeness and quality of total-dissolved-gas data, lower Columbia River, Oregon and Washington, water year 2012.

[TDG, total dissolved gas]

Abbreviated station name	Planned monitoring, (hours)	Number of missing or deleted hourly values	Percentage of real-time TDG data passing quality assurance criteria
John Day navigation lock (JDY)	4,516	19	99.6
John Day tailwater (JHAW)	8,784	11	99.9
The Dalles forebay (TDA)	4,552	0	100
The Dalles tailwater (TDDO)	8,784	12	99.9
Bonneville forebay (BON)	4,532	0	100
Cascade Island (CCIW)	4,703	1,042	77.8
Warrendale (WRNO)	8,784	3	100
Camas (CWMW)	4,285	46	98.9
Total	**48,940**	**1,133**	**97.7**

Periods for which substantial portions of TDG data are either missing from the database (for example, when data-collection instruments or structures failed) or for which data were later deleted from the database because they did not meet quality-assurance standards are listed in table 3.

Table 3. Periods of missing real-time total-dissolved-gas data, lower Columbia River, Oregon and Washington, water year 2012.

[USACE (U.S. Army Corps of Engineers) station identifier: JDY, John Day navigation lock; JHAW, John Day tailwater; TDDO, The Dalles tailwater; CCIW, Cascade Island; CWMW, Camas]

Date and Time	USACE station identifier	Reason / notes
3/21/12 and 3/22/12	JDY	Problems with the GOES satellite system. Data were received later.
Various dates	JHAW	Data gaps on several occasions due to routine calibration and to the rebuilding of the site.
Various dates	TDDO	Data loss due to routine calibration. Each loss was for one hourly value.
04/26/12 to 06/06/12	CCIW	Data were lost because the deployment pipe was destroyed by high water. The site was later rebuilt with a stronger pipe.
08/05/12 to 08/07/12	CWMW	TDG membrane was broken. Data could not be recovered.

The Cascade Island station had the most missing or deleted data. High discharge through the spillway destroyed the probe-enclosing pipe at the site on April 25, 2012. The probe was installed in a new pipe on June 6, 2012, and real-time TDG data collection resumed on that date. Prior to the new installation, a recording-only Hydrolab was placed at the site, and non-real-time data were collected for part of the time from May 31 to June 6, 2012.

Quality-Assurance Data

The collection of accurate data for TDG, barometric pressure, and water temperature involves several quality-assurance procedures, including side-by-side instrument comparisons in the field, sensor calibrations in the laboratory, daily checks of the data, and data review and archiving. These methods are explained in detail in Tanner and Johnston (2001). The results of the quality-assurance procedures for water year 2012 are presented in this section.

After field deployment for 3 or 4 weeks, the TDG instruments were calibrated in the laboratory. First, the sensor was tested, with the gas-permeable membrane in place, for response to supersaturated conditions. The membrane was then removed from the sensor and allowed to dry in a desiccator for 24 hours. Before the membrane was replaced, the TDG sensor was examined independently by comparing the reading of the TDG sensor to barometric pressure (100-percent saturation). Using a certified digital pressure gage (primary standard), comparisons also were made at pressures of 100, 200, and 300 mm Hg greater than barometric pressure (approximately 113-, 126-, and 139-percent saturation, respectively). The accuracy of the TDG sensors was calculated as the difference between the primary standard and the TDG sensor reading (expected minus actual) for each of the four test conditions divided by the barometric pressure and multiplied by 100 to obtain a percentage difference. Of the 98 laboratory checks that were performed on instruments after field deployment, all were within 0.7-percent saturation (fig. 2).

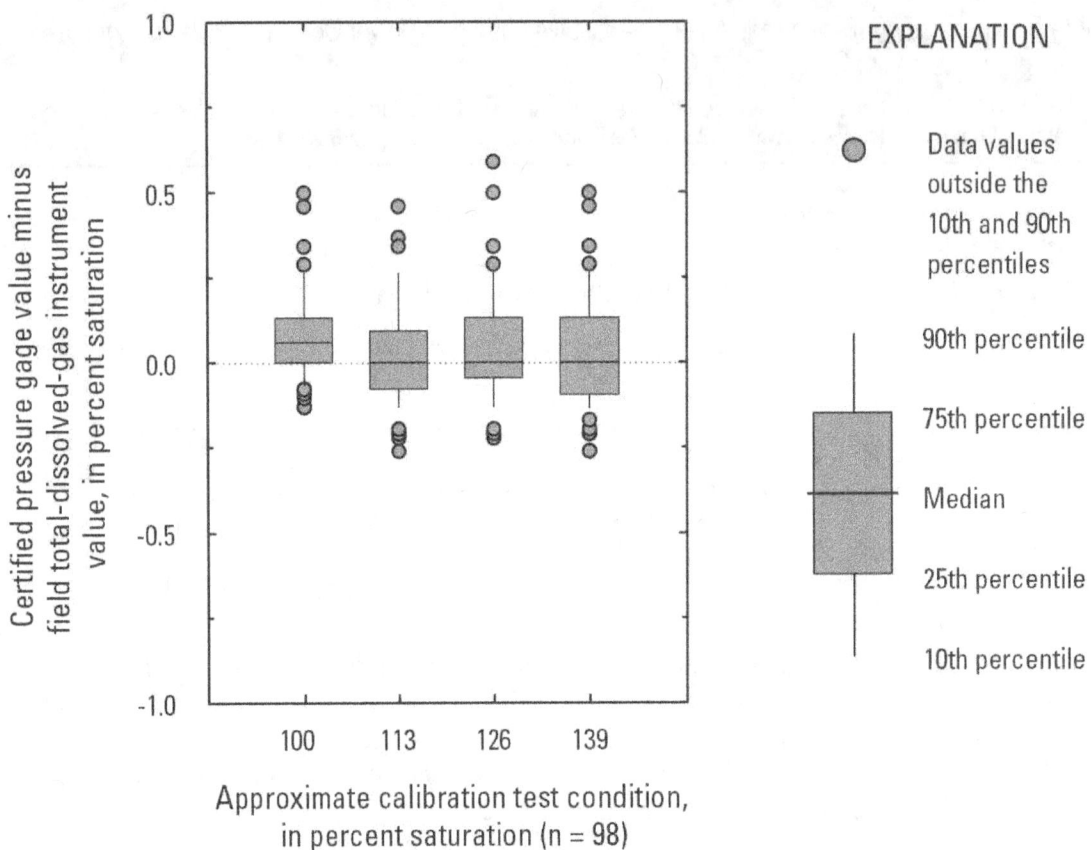

Figure 2. Boxplot showing accuracy of total-dissolved-gas sensors in the laboratory after 3 or 4 weeks of field deployment at eight monitoring stations in the lower Columbia River, Oregon and Washington, water year 2012 (number of comparison values = 98).

The differences in barometric pressure, onsite water temperature, and onsite TDG between the secondary standard instruments and the fixed-station monitors after field deployment were measured and recorded as part of every field inspection and calibration procedure. These differences, calculated as the secondary standard values minus the field instrument values, were used to compare and quantify the accuracy and precision between the two instruments. For water temperature and TDG, the measurements were made onsite with the secondary standard (a recently calibrated Hydrolab) positioned alongside the Hydrolab deployed in the river. A digital barometer, NIST-certified through April 2013, served as the primary standard for barometric pressure. The distribution of quality-assurance data for each of the three parameters from the eight stations is shown in figures 3, 4, and 5.

The comparisons of the digital barometer and the field barometers are shown in figure 3. All field values were within 1 mm Hg of standard values. The secondary standard temperature sensor and the field temperature sensor results are presented in figure 4. All differences were within 0.2°C.

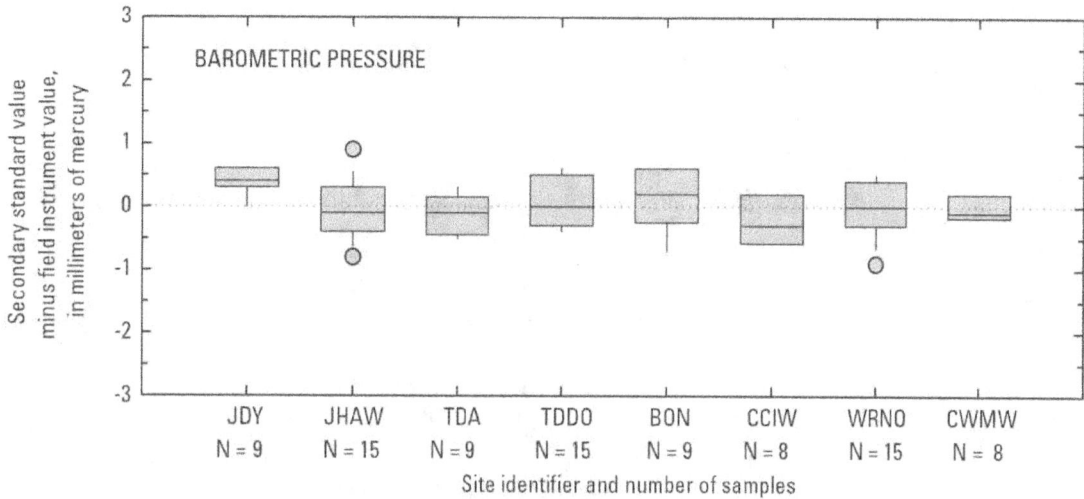

Figure 3.   Boxplot showing difference between the secondary standard and the field barometers in the field after 3 or 4 weeks of field deployment at eight stations in the lower Columbia River, Oregon and Washington, water year 2012. See figure 2 for explanation of boxplots.

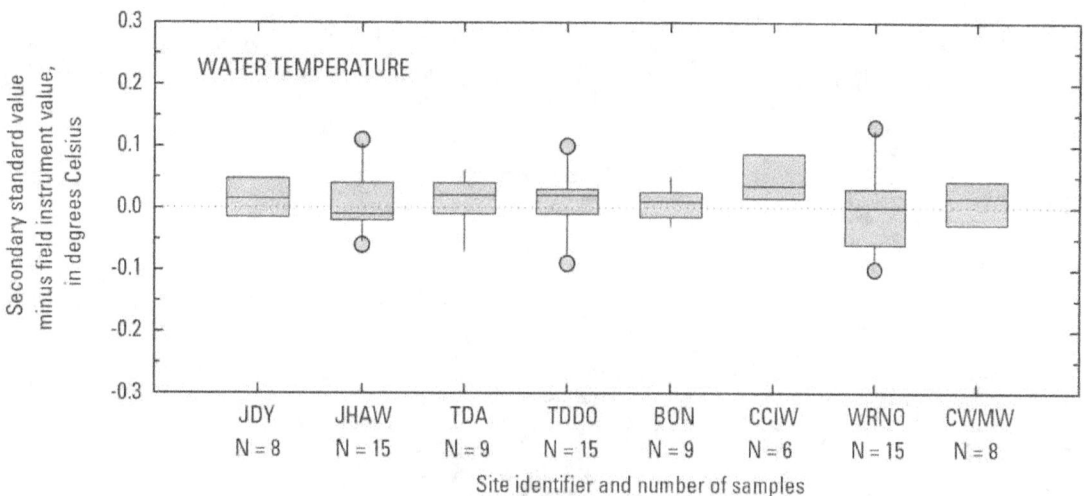

Figure 4.   Boxplot showing difference between the secondary standard and the field temperature instruments in the field after 3 or 4 weeks of field deployment at eight stations in the lower Columbia River, Oregon and Washington, water year 2012. See figure 2 for explanation of boxplots.

Differences between the secondary standard TDG sensor and the field TDG sensors were calculated following equilibration of the secondary standard unit to the site conditions before removing the field unit. The side-by-side equilibrium was considered complete after a minimum of 20 minutes when the TDG values for each sensor remained constant for 4–5 minutes. Only one of the field checks for TDG indicated a saturation difference greater than 1.0 percent (fig. 5).

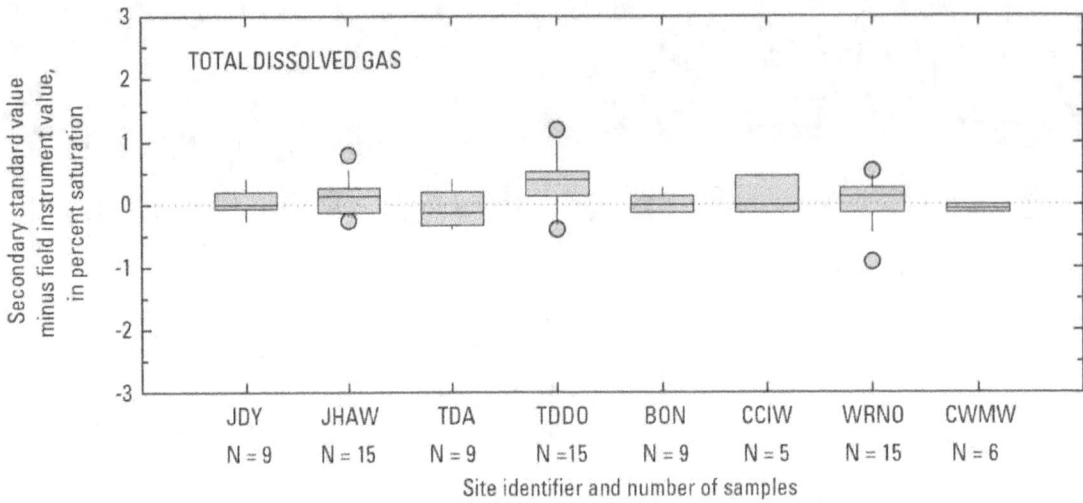

Figure 5. Boxplot showing difference between the secondary standard and the field total-dissolved-gas instruments in the field after 3 or 4 weeks of field deployment at eight stations in the lower Columbia River, Oregon and Washington, water year 2012. See figure 2 for explanation of boxplots.

Effects of Spill on Concentration of Total Dissolved Gas

The relations between spill rates at the dams and TDG at the corresponding tailwater site or sites were nearly linear for John Day Dam (fig. 6), The Dalles Dam (fig. 7), and Bonneville Dam (figs. 8 and 9).

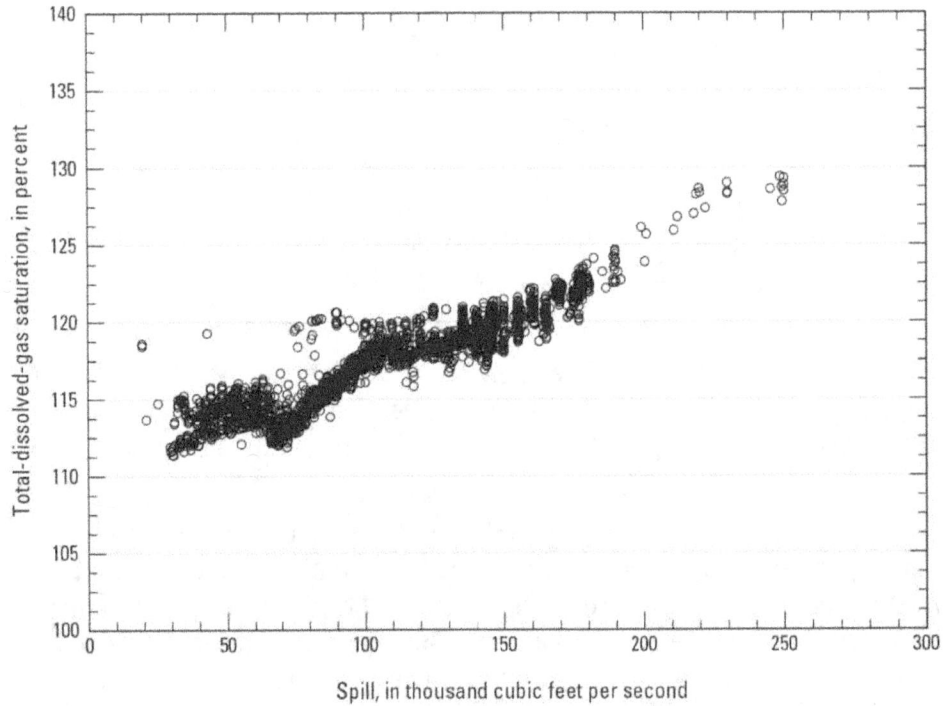

Figure 6. Graph showing relation of total-dissolved-gas saturation downstream of John Day Dam and spill from the dam, lower Columbia River, Oregon and Washington, April 1–August 31, 2012.

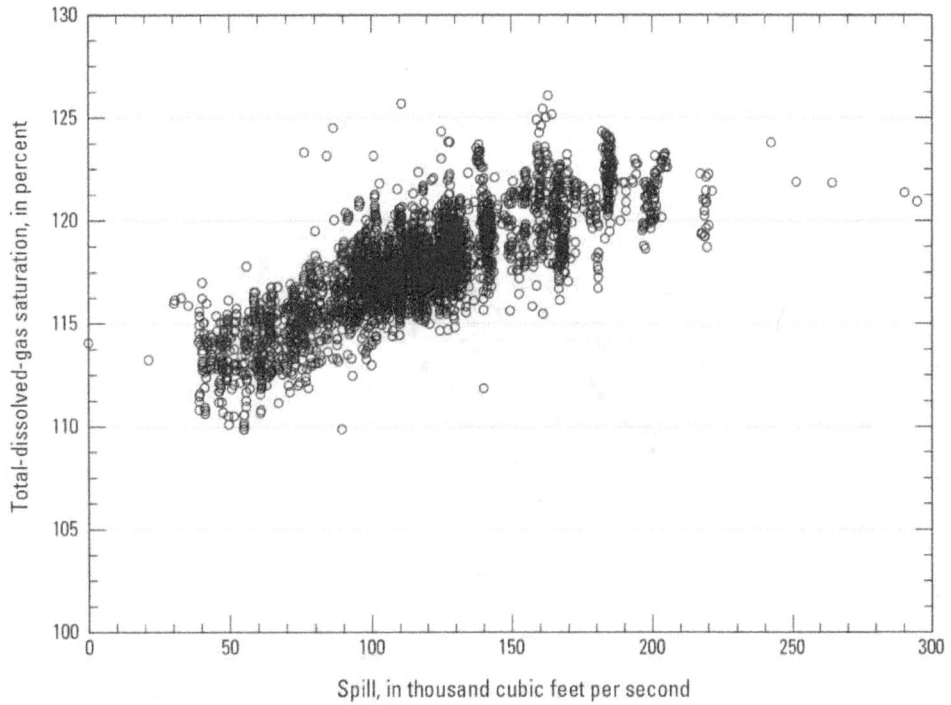

Figure 7. Graph showing relation of total-dissolved-gas saturation downstream of The Dalles Dam and spill from The Dalles Dam, lower Columbia River, Oregon and Washington, April 1–August 31, 2012.

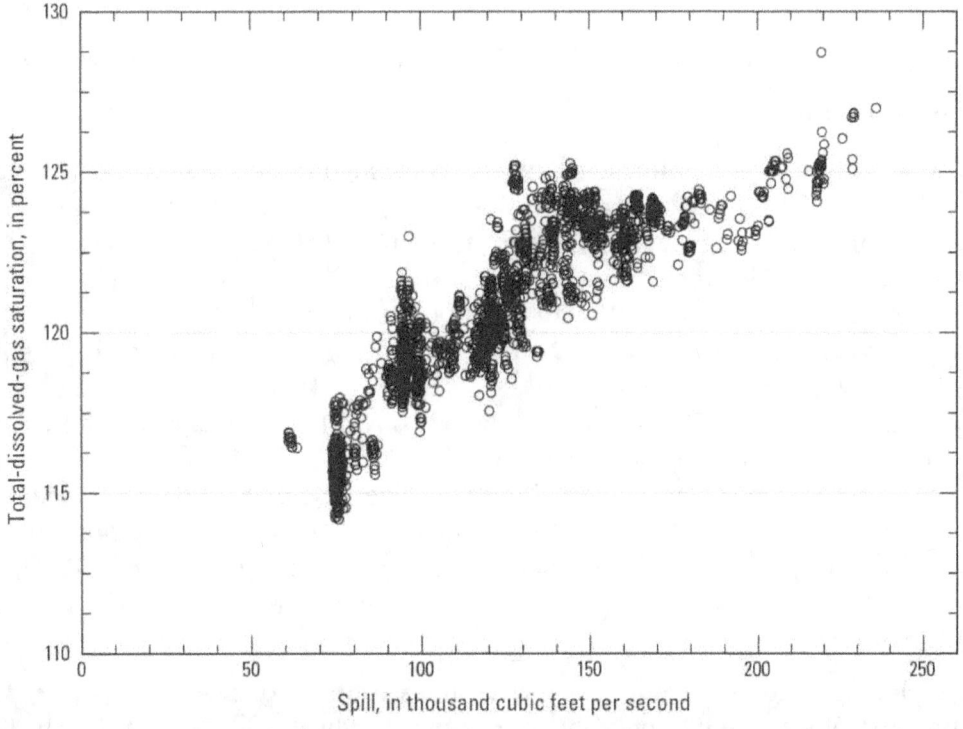

Figure 8. Graph showing relation of total-dissolved-gas saturation downstream of Bonneville Dam at Cascade Island and spill from Bonneville Dam, lower Columbia River, Oregon and Washington, April 1–August 31, 2012

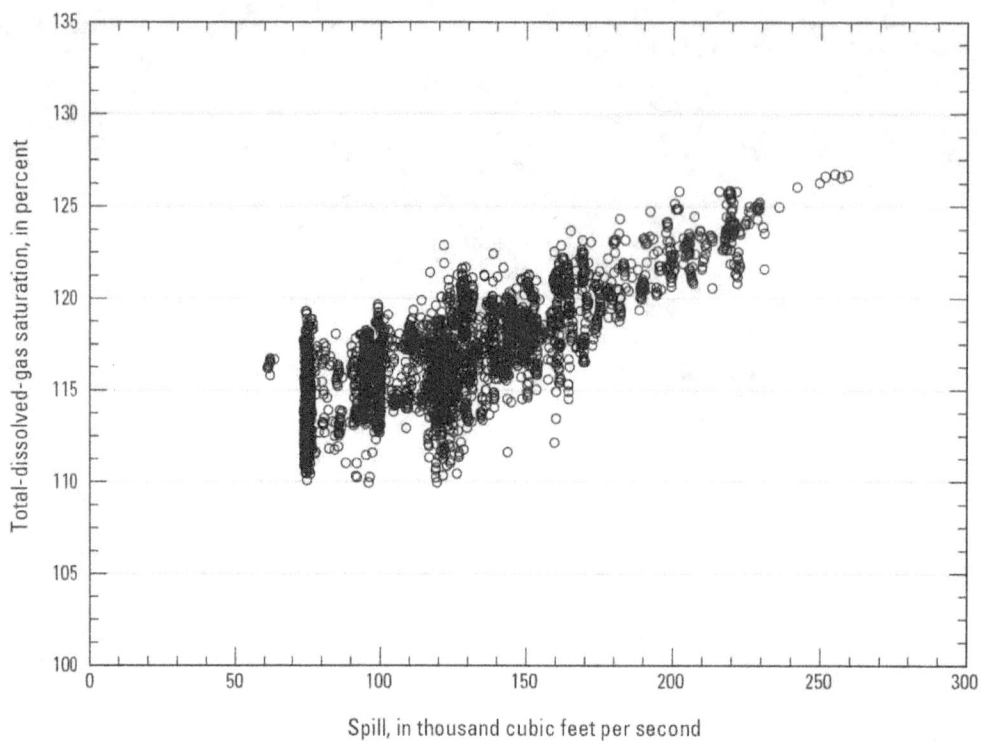

Figure 9. Graph showing relation of total-dissolved-gas saturation downstream of Bonne-ville Dam at Warrendale and spill from Bonneville Dam, lower Columbia River, Oregon and Washington, April 1–August 31, 2012

Comparison of Total-Dissolved-Gas Concentration and Water Temperature to Water-Quality Standards

In 2012, waivers (Oregon) or rule adjustments (Washington) were granted to the water-quality standard for TDG of 110-percent saturation to allow spill for fish passage at dams on the Columbia River. The State of Oregon granted a 5-year waiver for 2010–2014 (State of Oregon, 2009). The State of Washington provided for fish passage in its water-quality standards consistent with ap-proved gas-abatement plans (State of Washington, 2006a). From April 1 to August 31, 2012, the USACE was granted variances allowing TDG to reach 115-percent saturation at the forebay stations (John Day Dam navigation lock, The Dalles Dam forebay, and Bonneville Dam forebay) and Camas, and 120-percent saturation at tailwater stations, directly downstream of dams (John Day Dam tailwa-ter, The Dalles Dam tailwater, Cascade Island, and Warrendale). The 115- and 120-percent variances were exceeded if the average of the highest 12-hourly values in 1 day (1:00 a.m. to midnight) (Ore-gon waiver) or the average of the 12 highest consecutive hourly readings in any 24-hour period (Washington rule adjustment) were larger than the variance. A separate variance of 125 percent was established for all stations for either the highest 2-hour average (Oregon Environmental Quality Commission, written commun., 2007), or the highest 1-hour average (State of Washington, 2006a).

The distribution of hourly TDG values for the spill season in 2012 (April 1–August 31, 2012) is shown in figure 10 along with the applicable waiver or rule adjustment for each station. The waivers or rule adjustments apply to an average value, whereas the distribution plots show the hourly values. Consequently, the points representing values greater than the Oregon and Washington standards (shown as lines on the graph) do not necessarily represent actual exceedances of the standards.

12

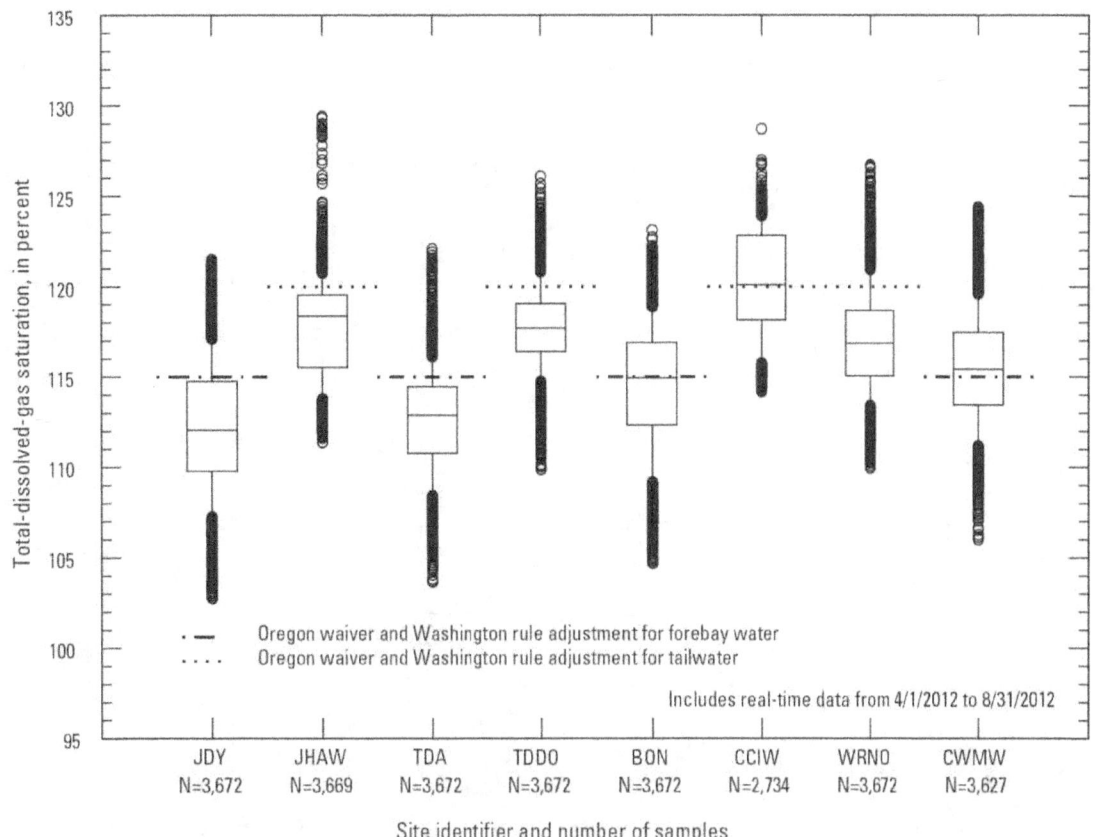

Figure 10. Boxplot showing distributions of hourly total-dissolved-gas data and Oregon and Washington total-dissolved-gas waivers/rule adjustments, lower Columbia River, Oregon and Washington, April 1–August 31, 2012. See figure 2 for explanation of boxplots.

The timing of the occurrence of exceedances of TDG standards (high 12-hour daily average for comparison to the Oregon waiver) and the timing of the spill at the closest upstream dam are shown in figures 11–18. For the calculations of the high 12-hour average, missing TDG data were ignored and the next adjacent data points were used to calculate whether an exceedance had occurred. For each site, the TDG standards were exceeded for part of the time during April, May, June, and July 2012.

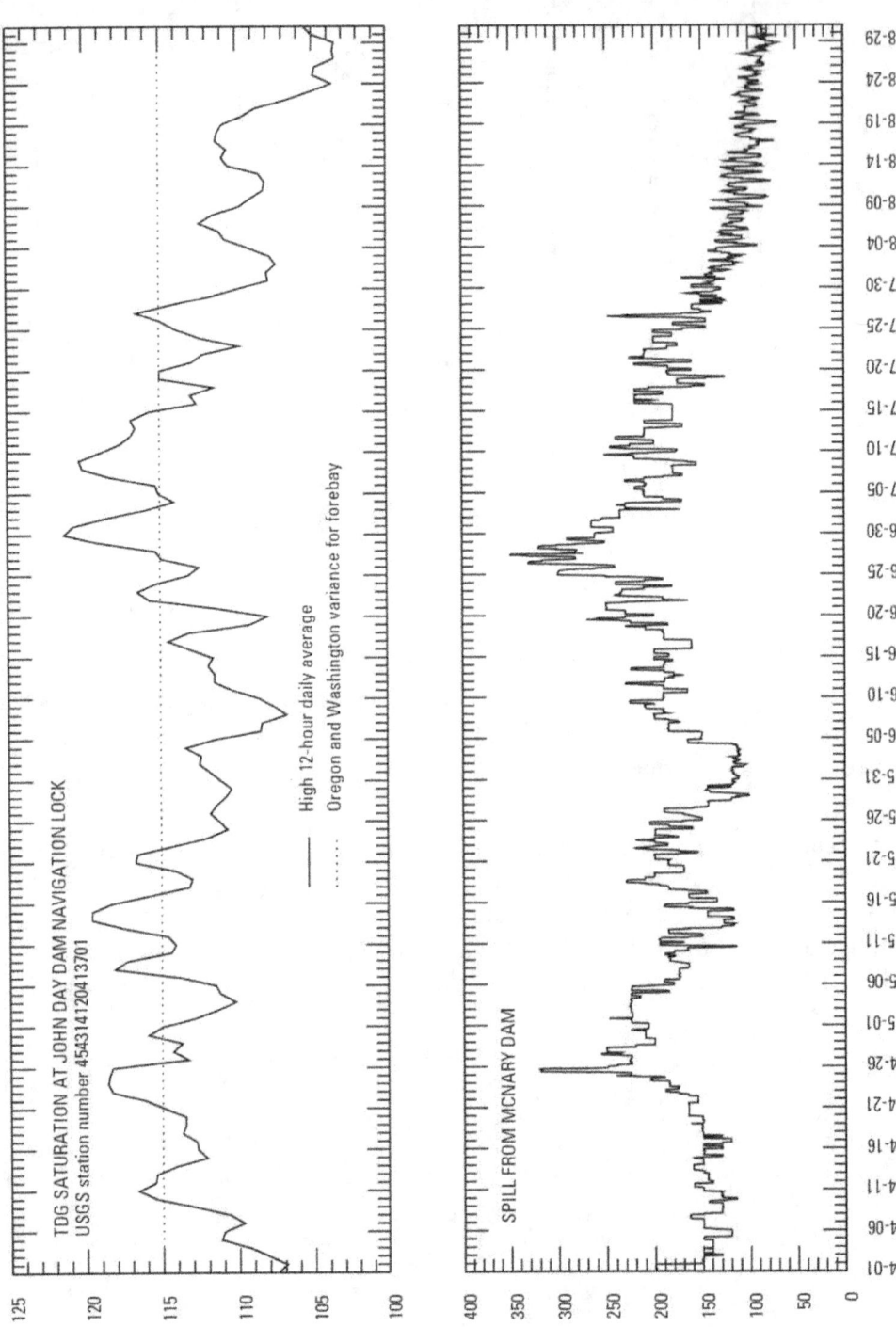

Figure 11. Graphs showing high 12-hour average of total-dissolved-gas saturation at John Day Dam navigation lock and spill from McNary Dam (76 river miles upstream from John Day Dam), lower Columbia River, Oregon and Washington, April 1–August 31, 2012.

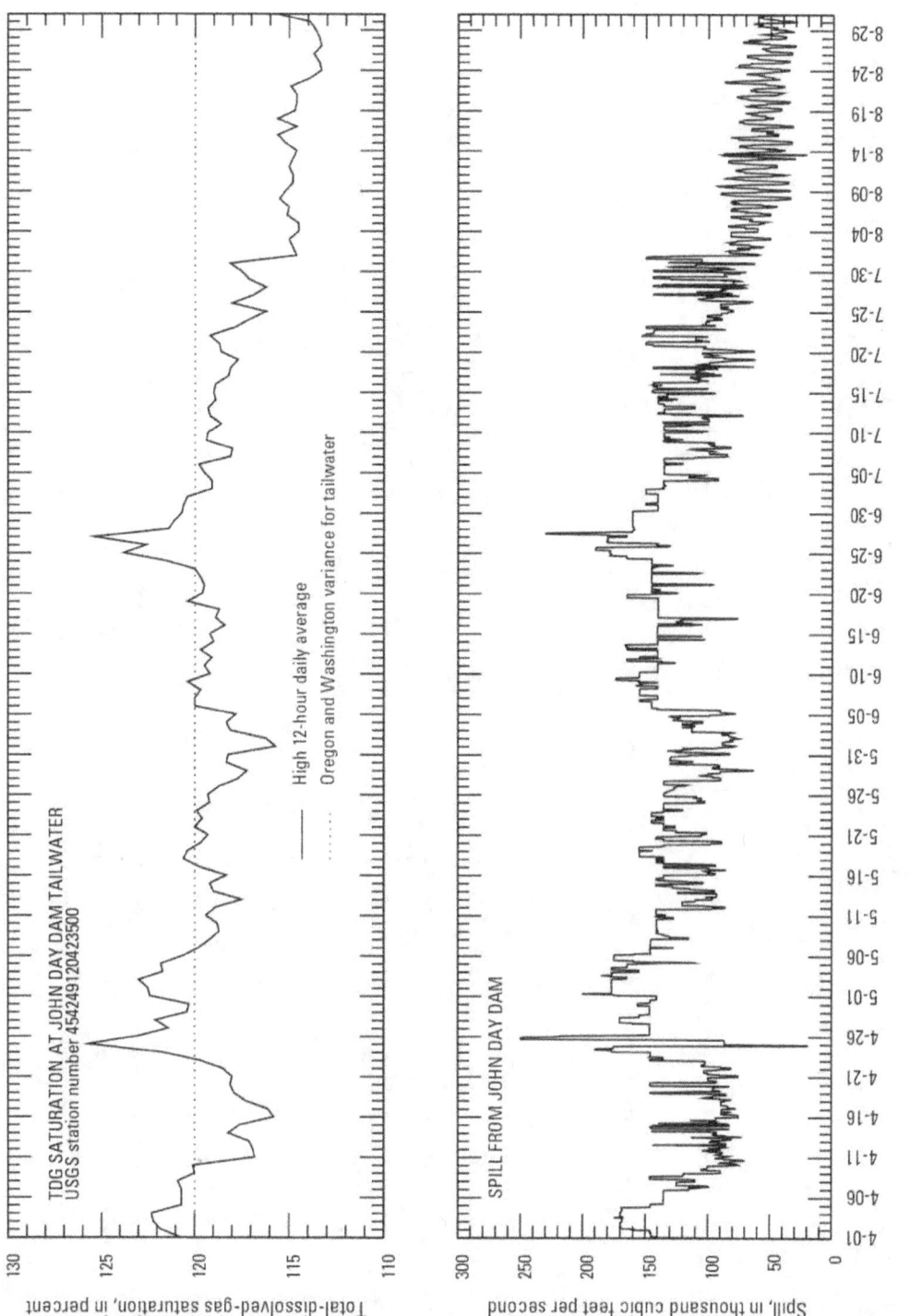

Figure 12. Graphs showing total-dissolved-gas saturation at John Day Dam tailwater and spill from John Day Dam, lower Columbia River, Oregon and Washington, April 1–August 31, 2012.

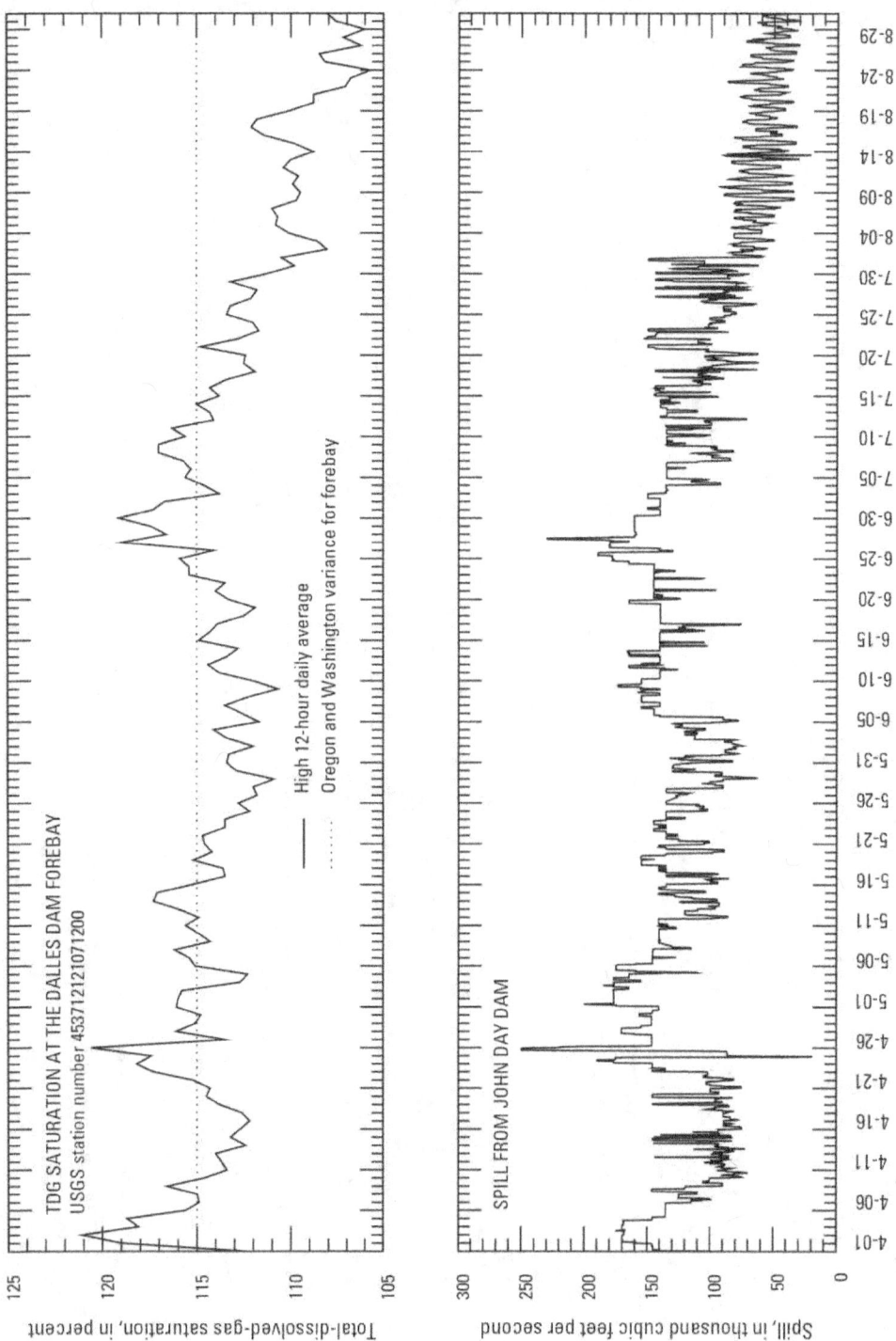

Figure 13. Graphs showing total-dissolved-gas saturation at The Dalles Dam forebay and spill from John Day Dam, lower Columbia River, Oregon and Washington, April 1–August 31, 2012.

16

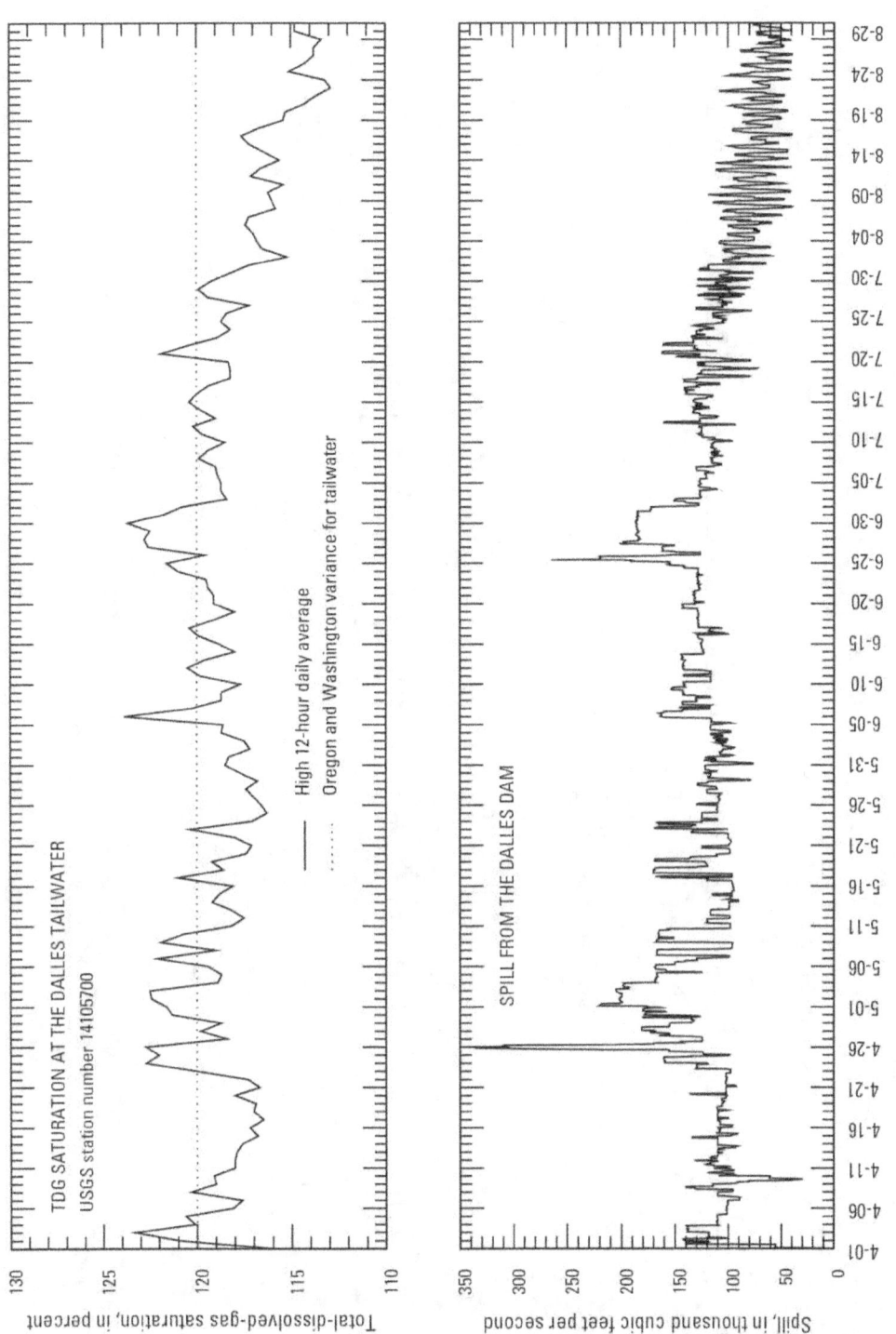

Figure 14. Graphs showing total-dissolved-gas saturation at The Dalles Dam tailwater and spill from The Dalles Dam, lower Columbia River, Oregon and Washington, April 1–August 31, 2012.

17

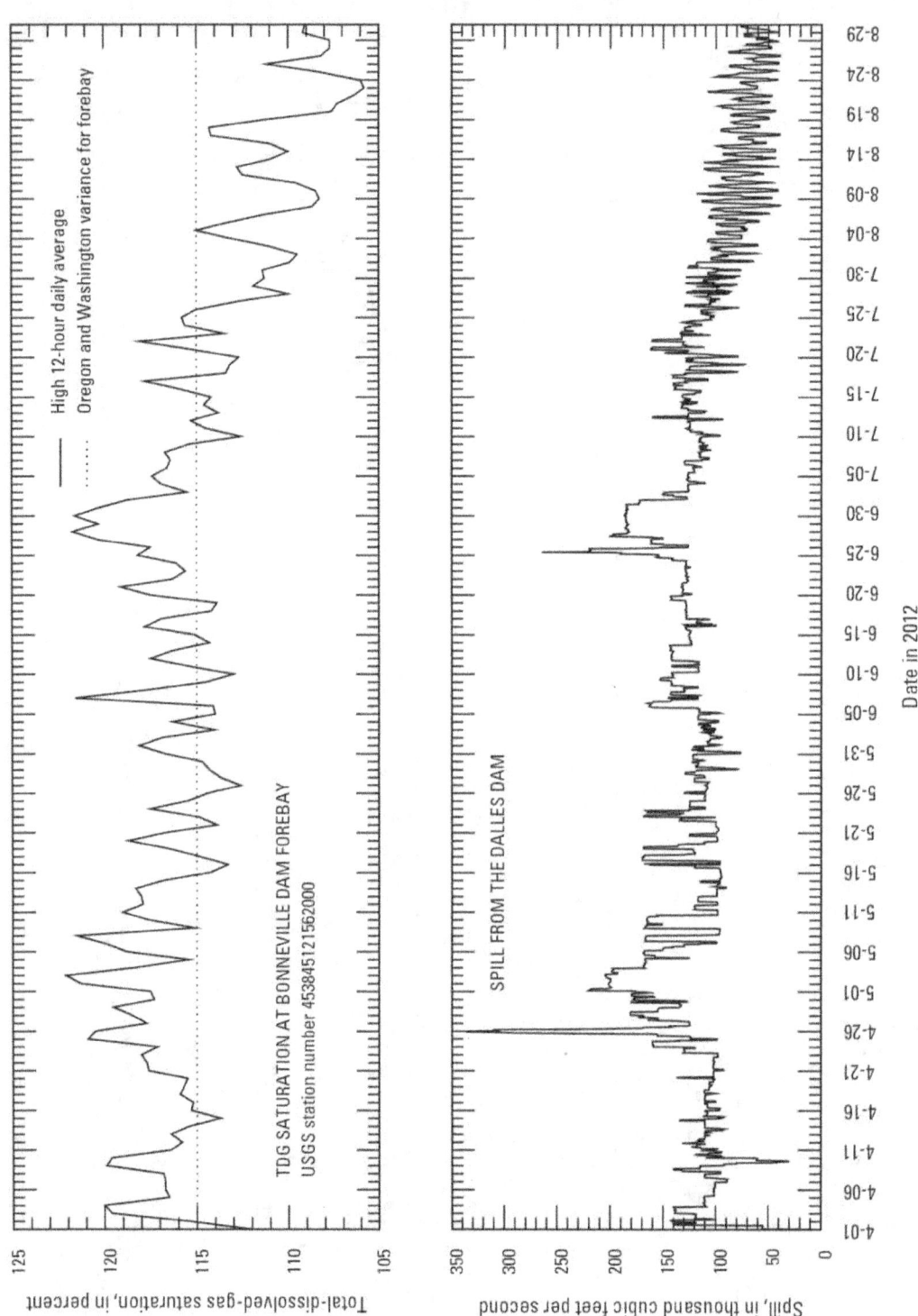

Figure 15. Graphs showing total-dissolved-gas saturation at Bonneville Dam forebay and spill from The Dalles Dam, lower Columbia River, Oregon and Washington, April 1–August 31, 2012.

18

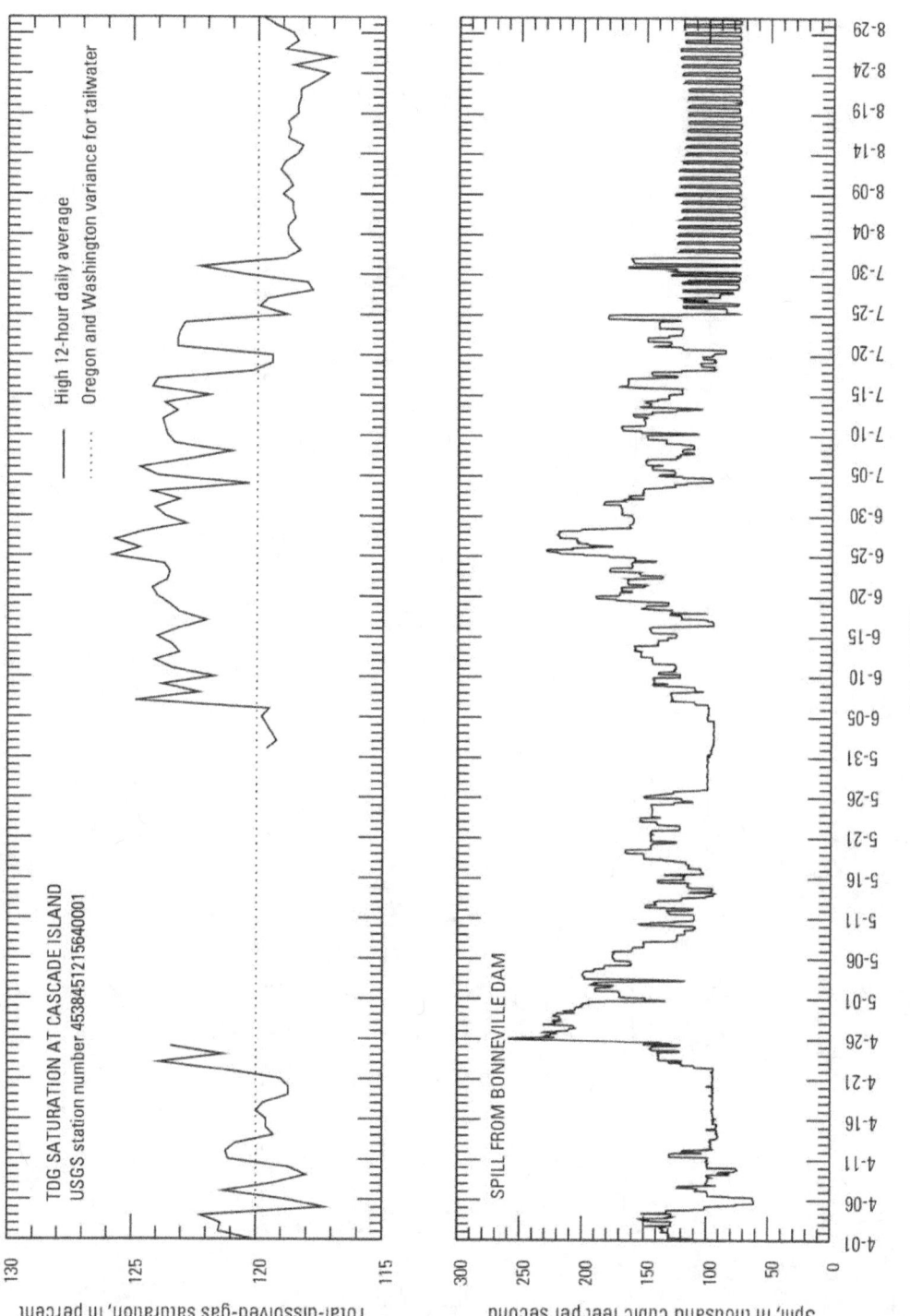

Figure 16. Graphs showing total-dissolved-gas saturation at Cascade Island and spill from Bonneville Dam, lower Columbia River, Oregon and Washington, April 1–August 31, 2012

19

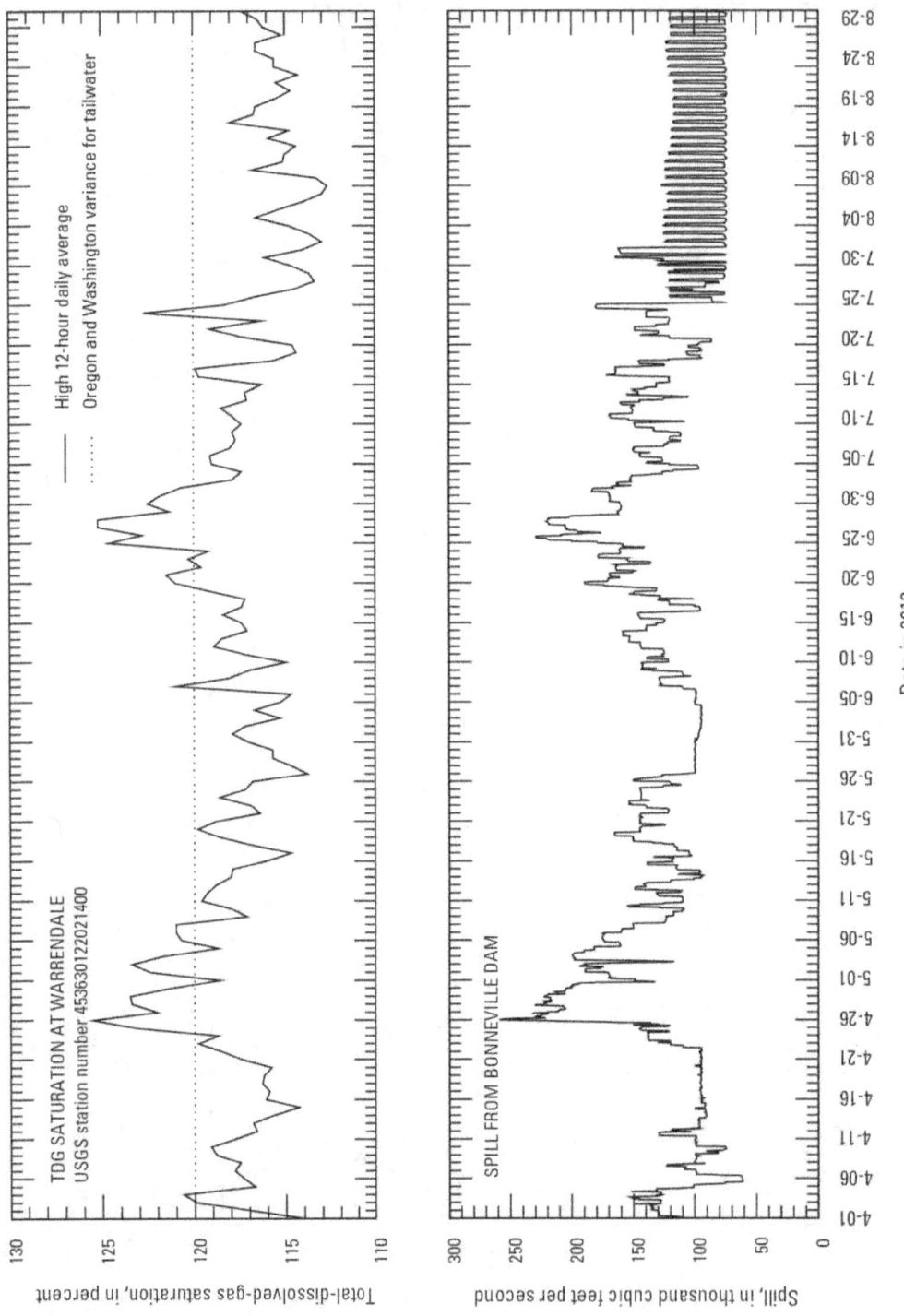

Figure 17. Graphs showing total-dissolved-gas saturation at Warrendale and spill from Bonneville Dam, lower Columbia River, Oregon and Washington, April 1–August 31, 2012

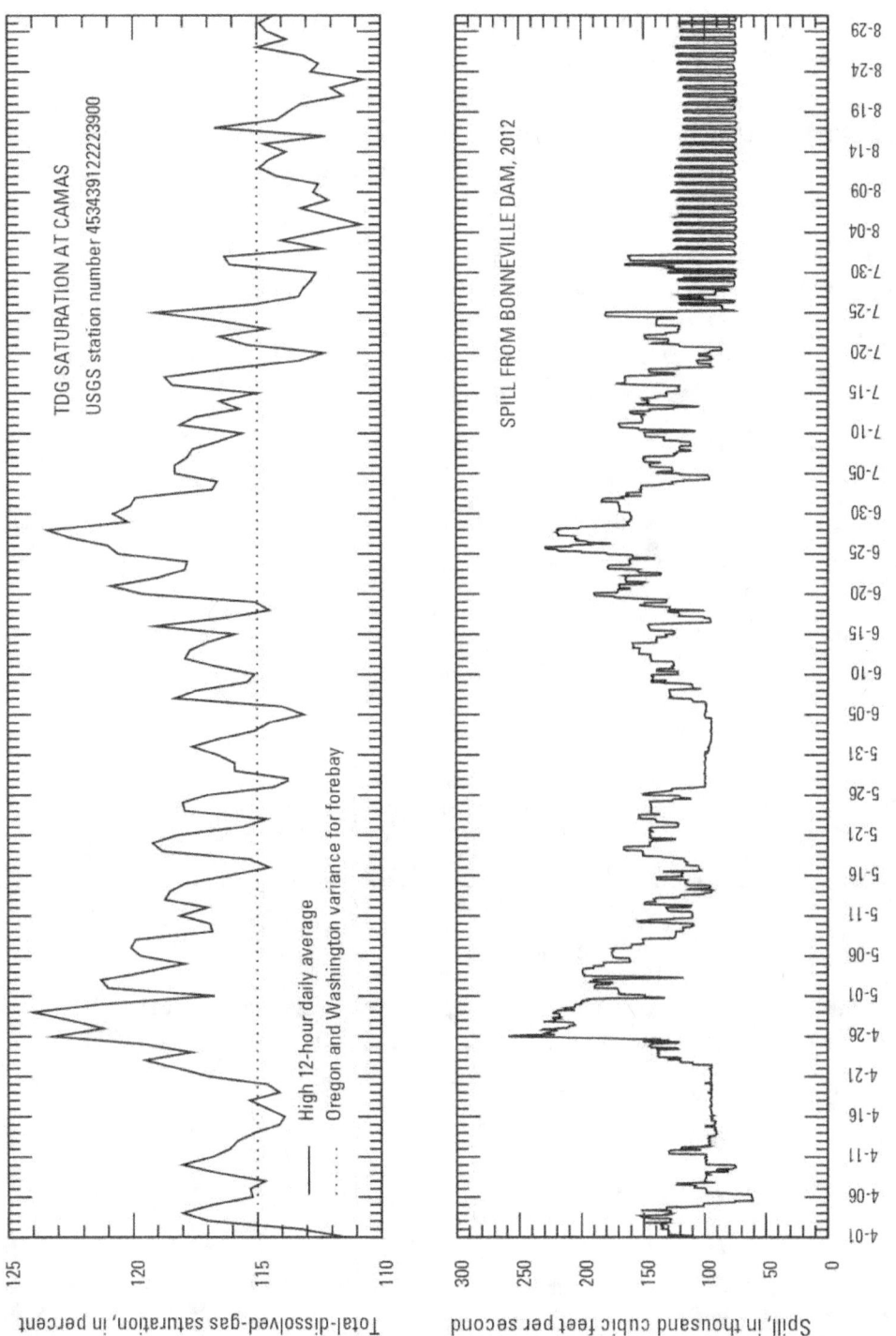

Figure 18. Graphs showing total-dissolved-gas saturation at Camas and spill from Bonneville Dam, lower Columbia River, Oregon and Washington, April 1–August 31, 2012

Water-temperature standards that apply to the lower Columbia River are complex and depend on the effects of human activities and the locations of salmonid rearing, spawning, and egg incubation areas. According to the State of Oregon water-temperature standard, the 7-day-average of the daily maximum temperature of the lower Columbia River should not exceed 20°C (State of Oregon, 2008). Washington State regulations mandate that the water temperature in the Columbia River shall not exceed a 1-day maximum of 20.0°C due to human activities (State of Washington, 2006b).

This report addresses only the hourly values for water temperature. Water temperatures at all sites were greater than 20.0°C during parts of August and September (figs. 19–23). Water temperatures at the forebay stations were approximately equal to the temperatures at the tailwater stations (except during short time periods at the John Day Dam).

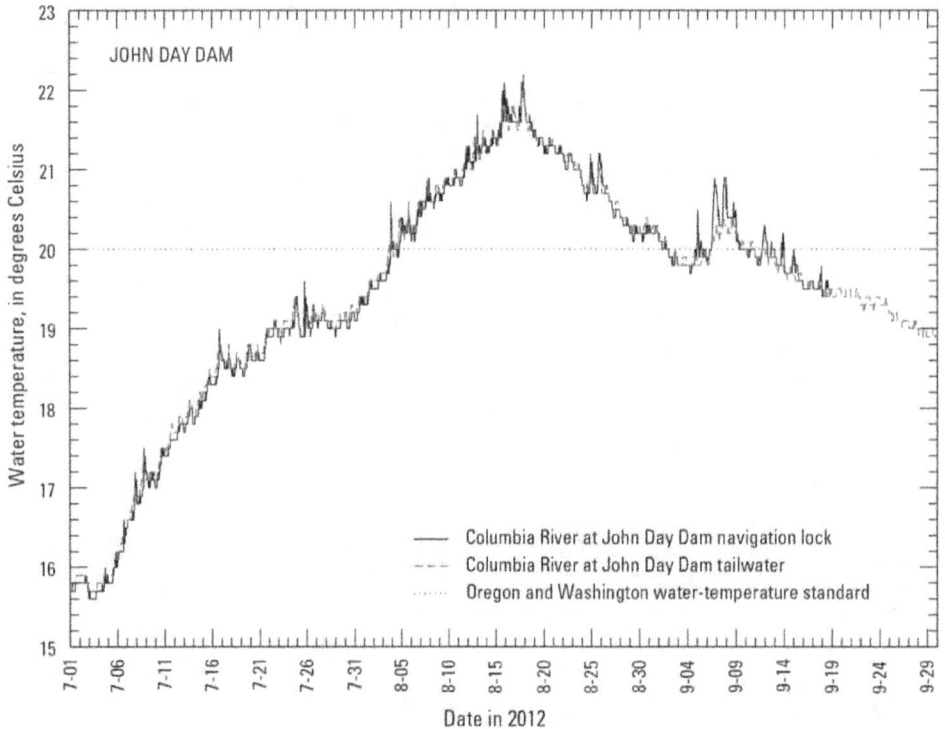

Figure 19. Graph showing water temperature upstream of John Day Dam and downstream of John Day Dam, lower Columbia River, Oregon and Washington, summer 2012.

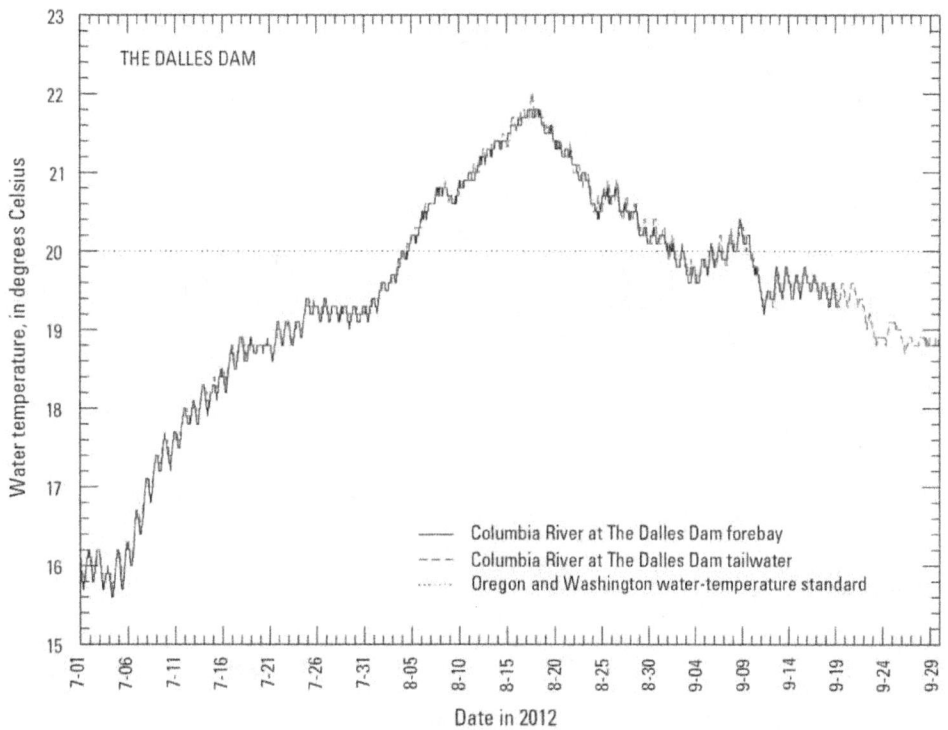

Figure 20. Graph showing water temperature upstream and downstream of The Dalles Dam, lower Columbia River, Oregon and Washington, summer 2012.

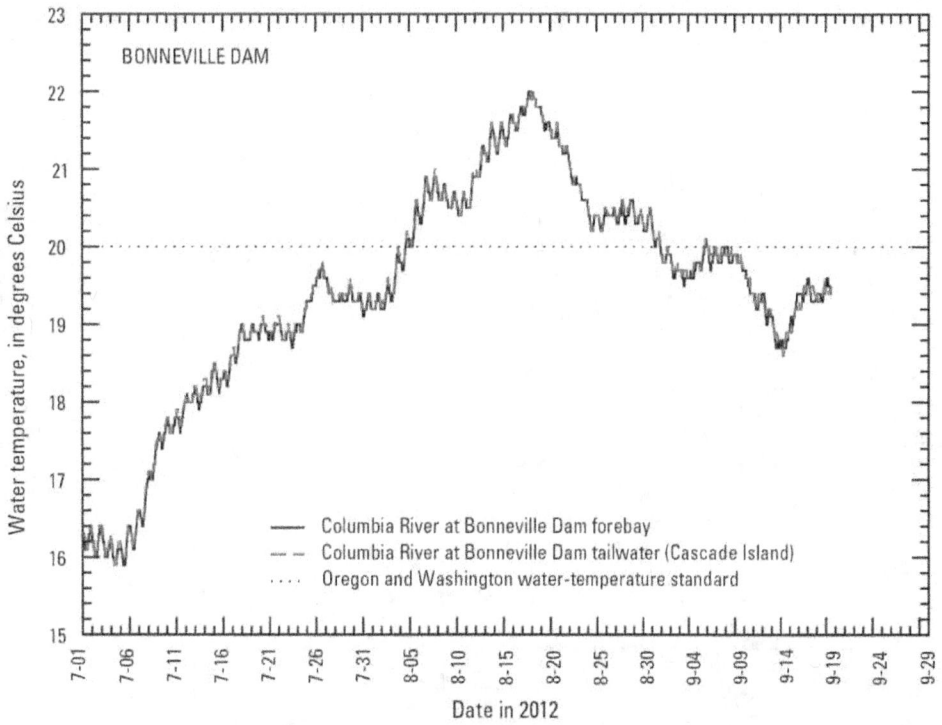

Figure 21. Graph showing water temperature upstream of Bonneville Dam and downstream of Bonneville Dam at Cascade Island, lower Columbia River, Oregon and Washington, summer 2012

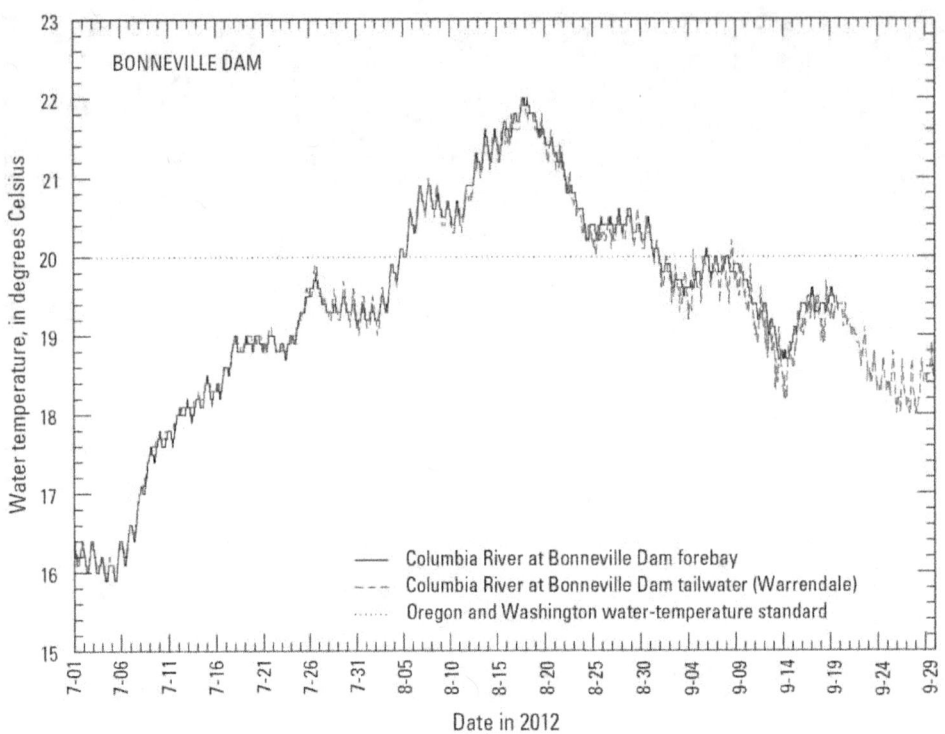

Figure 22. Graph showing water temperature upstream of Bonneville Dam and downstream of Bonneville Dam at Warrendale, lower Columbia River, Oregon and Washington, summer 2012.

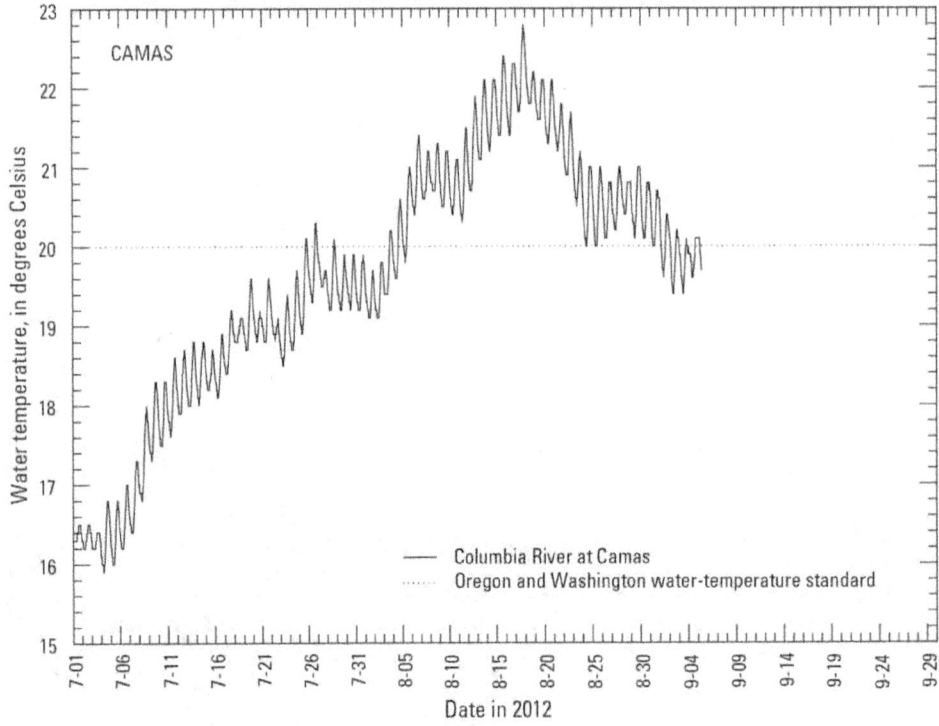

Figure 23. Graph showing water temperature downstream of Bonneville Dam at Camas, lower Columbia River, Oregon and Washington, summer 2012.

Acknowledgments

The authors extend special thanks to Tina Lundell (USACE) for technical and logistical support of the project. The authors also thank Amy M. Brooks (USGS) for analyzing and preparing summaries of the data.

References Cited

Colt, J., 1984, Computation of dissolved gas concentrations in water as functions of temperature, salinity, and pressure: American Fisheries Society Special Publication 14, 154 p.

Jones, J.C., Tracey, D.C., and Sorensen, F.W., eds., 1991, Operating manual for the U.S. Geological Survey's data-collection system with the Geostationary Operational Environmental Satellite: U.S. Geological Survey Open-File Report 91–99, 237 p. (Also available at http://pubs.usgs.gov/of/1991/0099/.)

State of Oregon, 2009, Order approving the U.S. Army Corps of Engineer's [sic] request for a waiver to the State's total dissolved gas water quality standard: Oregon Department of Environmental Quality, 4 p., accessed February 15, 2013, at *http://www.deq.state.or.us/WQ/TMDLs/docs/columbiariver/tdg/USACEWaiiver2010.pdf*.

State of Oregon, 2008, Water quality standards—Beneficial uses, policies, and criteria for Oregon: Oregon Department of Environmental Quality, accessed February 15, 2013, at *http://arcweb.sos.state.or.us/pages/rules/oars_300/oar_340/340_041.html*.

State of Washington, 2006a, Fresh water designated uses and criteria–Aquatic life total dissolved gas (TDG) criteria, WAC 173–201A–200(1)(f): Washington State Legislature Web site, accessed February 15, 2013, at *http://apps.leg.wa.gov/WAC/default.aspx?cite=173-201A-200*.

State of Washington, 2006b, Water quality standards for surface waters of the State of Washington: State of Washington, 103 p., accessed February 15, 2013, at *http://www.ecy.wa.gov/pubs/wac173201a.pdf*.

Tanner, D.Q., and Bragg, H.M., 2001, Quality-assurance data, comparison to water-quality standards, and site considerations for total dissolved gas and water temperature, lower Columbia River, Oregon and Washington, 2001: U.S. Geological Survey Water-Resources Investigations Report 2001–4273, 14 p. (Also available at *http://or.water.usgs.gov/pubs_dir/WRIR01-4273/.*)

Tanner, D.Q., Bragg, H.M., and Johnston, M.W., 2003, Total dissolved gas and water temperature in the Lower Columbia River, Oregon and Washington, 2003—Quality-assurance data and comparison to water-quality standards: U.S. Geological Survey Water-Resources Investigations Report 2003–4306, 24 p. (Also available at *http://pubs.usgs.gov/wri/wri034306/.*)

Tanner, D.Q., Bragg, H.M., and Johnston, M.W., 2004, Total dissolved gas and water temperature in the Lower Columbia River, Oregon and Washington, 2004—Quality-assurance data and comparison to water-quality standards: U.S. Geological Survey Scientific Investigations Report 2004–5249, 27 p. (Also available at *http://pubs.usgs.gov/sir/2004/5249/.*)

Tanner, D.Q., Bragg, H.M., and Johnston, M.W., 2005, Total dissolved gas and water temperature in the Lower Columbia River, Oregon and Washington, 2005—Quality-assurance data and comparison to water-quality standards: U.S. Geological Survey Data Series 148, 31 p. (Also available at *http://pubs.usgs.gov/ds/2005/148/.*)

Tanner, D.Q., Bragg, H.M., and Johnston, M.W., 2006, Total dissolved gas and water temperature in the Lower Columbia River, Oregon and Washington, 2006—Quality-assurance data and comparison to water-quality standards: U.S. Geological Survey Data Series 235, 24 p. (Also available at *http://pubs.usgs.gov/ds/2006/235/.*)

Tanner, D.Q., Bragg, H.M., and Johnston, M.W., 2007, Total dissolved gas and water temperature in the Lower Columbia River, Oregon and Washington, 2007—Quality-assurance data and comparison to water-quality standards: U.S. Geological Survey Open-File Report 2007–1408, 23 p. (Also available at *http://pubs.usgs.gov/of/2007/1408/.*)

Tanner, D.Q., Bragg, H.M., and Johnston, M.W., 2008, Total dissolved gas and water temperature in the Lower Columbia River, Oregon and Washington, 2008—Quality-assurance data and comparison to water-quality standards: U.S. Geological Survey Open-File Report 2008–1357, 25 p. (Also available at *http://pubs.usgs.gov/of/2008/1357/.*)

Tanner, D.Q., Bragg, H.M., and Johnston, M.W., 2009, Total dissolved gas and water temperature in the Lower Columbia River, Oregon and Washington, 2009—Quality-assurance data and comparison to water-quality standards: U.S. Geological Survey Open-File Report 2009–1288, 26 p. (Also available at *http://pubs.usgs.gov/of/2009/1288/.*)

Tanner, D.Q., Bragg, H.M., and Johnston, M.W., 2011, Total dissolved gas and water temperature in the Lower Columbia River, Oregon and Washington, 2010—Quality-assurance data and comparison to water-quality standards: U.S. Geological Survey Open-File Report 2011–1293, 28 p. (Also available at *http://pubs.usgs.gov/of/2010/1293/.*)

Tanner, D.Q., Bragg, H.M., and Johnston, M.W., 2012, Total dissolved gas and water temperature in the lower Columbia River, Oregon and Washington, water year 2011—Quality-assurance data and comparison to water-quality standards: U.S. Geological Survey Open-File Report 2011–1300, 28 p. (Also available at *http://pubs.usgs.gov/of/2011/1300.*)

Tanner, D.Q., Harrison, H.E., and McKenzie, S.W., 1996, Total dissolved gas, barometric pressure, and water temperature data, lower Columbia River, Oregon and Washington, 1996: U.S. Geological Survey Open-File Report 96–662A, 85 p. (Also available at *http://or.water.usgs.gov/pubs_dir/Abstracts/96-662a.html.*)

Tanner, D.Q. and Johnston, M.W., 2001, Data-collection methods, quality-assurance data, and site considerations for total dissolved gas monitoring, lower Columbia River, Oregon and Washington, 2000: U.S. Geological Survey Water-Resources Investigations Report 2001–4005, 19 p. (Available at *http://or.water.usgs.gov/pubs_dir/Abstracts/01-4005.html.*)

Tanner, D.Q., Johnston, M.W., and Bragg, H.M., 2002, Total dissolved gas and water temperature in the Lower Columbia River, Oregon and Washington, 2002—Quality-assurance data and comparison to water-quality standards: U.S. Geological Survey Water-Resources Investigations Report 2002--4283, 12 p. (Available at *http://or.water.usgs.gov/pubs_dir/WRIR02-4283/.*)

U.S. Army Corps of Engineers, 2012, Total dissolved gas reports: U.S. Army Corps of Engineers, Columbia Basin Water Management Division Web site, accessed February 15, 2013, at *http://www.nwd-wc.usace.army.mil/tmt/wcd/tdg/months.html.*

U.S. Environmental Protection Agency, 1986, Quality criteria for water 1986: U.S. Environmental Protection Agency Publication No. 440-5-86-001, accessed February 15, 2013, at *http://water.epa.gov/scitech/swguidance/standards/criteria/aqlife/upload/2009_01_13_criteria_goldbook.pdf.*

www.ingramcontent.com/pod-product-compliance
Lightning Source LLC
Chambersburg PA
CBHW080356290526
45791CB00009BA/2889